EXCAVATORS
ON THE JOB

RYAN JAMES

Cataloging-in-Publication Data

Names: James, Ryan.
Title: Excavators on the job / Ryan James.
Description: Buffalo, NY : Norwood House Press, 2026. | Series: Big machines for big jobs | Includes glossary and index.
Identifiers: ISBN 9781978573819 (pbk.) | ISBN 9781978573826 (library bound) | ISBN 9781978573833 (ebook)
Subjects: LCSH: Excavating machinery--Juvenile literature.
Classification: LCC TA735.J359 2026 | DDC 621.8'65--dc23

Published in 2026 by
Norwood House Press
2544 Clinton Street
Buffalo, NY 14224

Find us on 

TABLE OF CONTENTS

PARTS OF AN EXCAVATOR

Excavators are big machines. **Tracks** help them move on rough ground.

5

Excavators have a cab. The **operator** sits there. The **boom** rises above the cab.

The arm connects to the boom. At the end of the arm is the bucket.

WHAT DOES AN EXCAVATOR DO?

Excavators work on **construction** sites. They dig. They scoop and lift. They move dirt, rocks, and other **materials**.

The operator **controls** the arm. The arm moves the bucket into place.

The bucket is lowered. It has sharp teeth on its edge. It digs deep into the ground.

The bucket gets a big scoop of dirt or other material. The operator drives the excavator to a new spot. The bucket unloads.

Excavators do many jobs. They **mine** the earth. They knock down old buildings.

Excavators can clear trees from land.

They can **dredge** rivers.

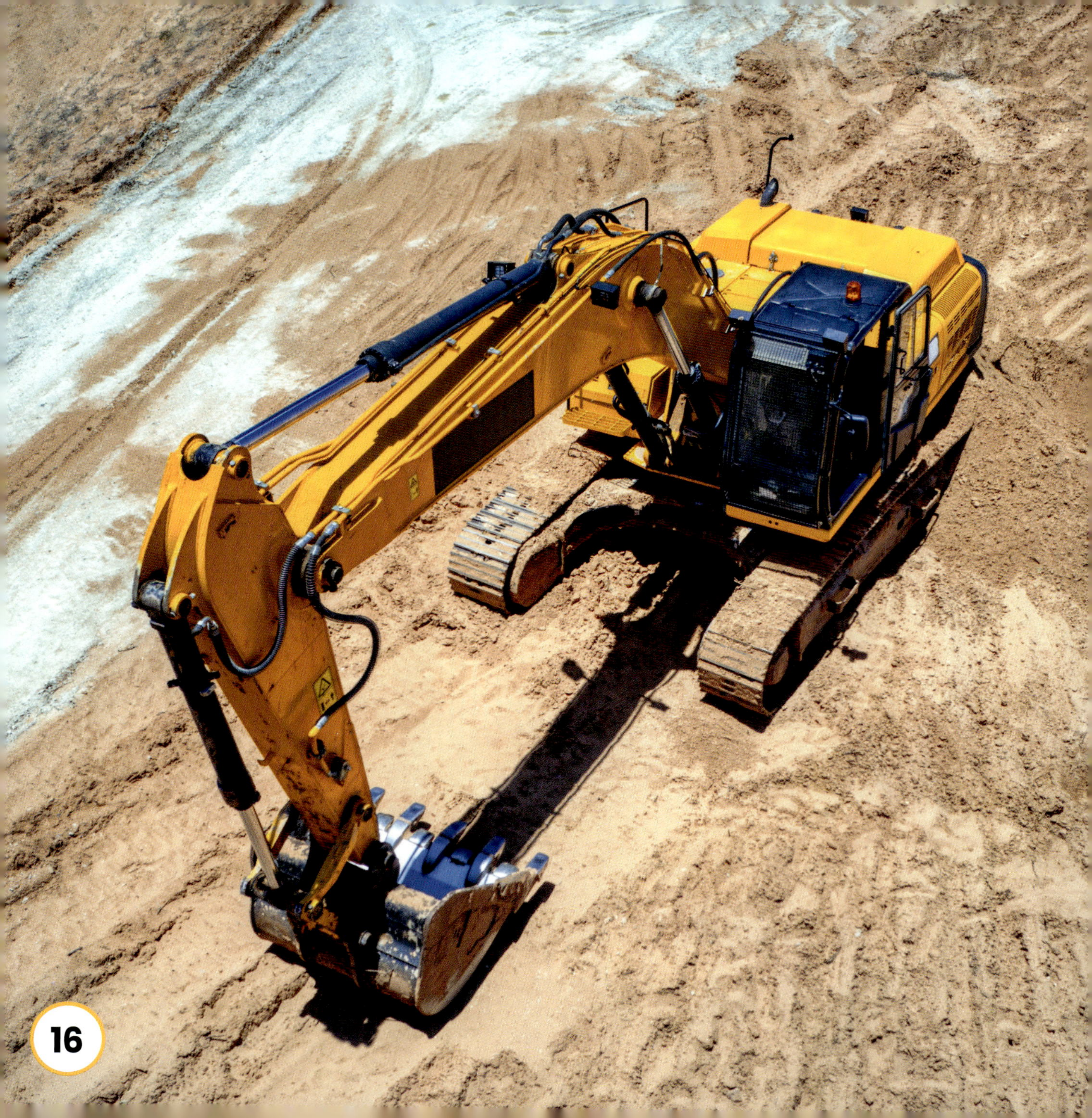

EXCAVATOR SAFETY

Be careful around an excavator.

Sharp, moving parts can hurt you.

Listen to an adult. Do not go near an excavator without **permission**.

18

The operator has an important job.

Do not bother them while they work.

EXCAVATORS IN ACTION

Excavators are **vehicles** on the job. They help get things done on construction sites!

GLOSSARY

boom (boom): the long brace that supports an excavator's arm and bucket

construction (kuhn-STRUHK-shuhn): related to building houses, roads, and other structures

controls (kuhn-TROHLZ): makes a machine work by pushing buttons and moving levers and switches

dredge (drej): to scrape the bottom of a body of water to make it deeper

materials (muh-TEER-ee-uhlz): things needed for a project, such as rocks, dirt, or bricks

mine (mine): to dig up minerals and other valuable materials from the ground

operator (AH-puh-ray-tur): a person whose job is to work a machine

permission (pur-MISH-uhn): being told it is okay to do something

tracks (traks): looping belts that help a vehicle move over rough ground

vehicles (VEE-i-kuhlz): machines used to move people or things from one place to another

THINKING QUESTIONS

1. What is the job of an excavator?

2. What does an excavator operator do?

3. What projects can an excavator do?

4. How can you stay safe around an excavator?

5. Why is an excavator important?

INDEX

ABOUT THE AUTHOR

Ryan James lives in the mountains of North Carolina where he goes hiking with his dog Bailey. He loves fly fishing, visiting farms in the area, and picking fresh produce. He has always enjoyed writing and wrote his first book as a teenager.